Cars

Carmel Reilly

Nelson Thornes

Nelson Thornes

First published in 2007 by Cengage Learning Australia
www.cengage.com.au

This edition published in 2008 under the imprint of Nelson Thornes Ltd,
Delta Place, 27 Bath Road, Cheltenham, United Kingdom, GL53 7TH

10 9 8 7 6 5 4 3 2
11 10 09 08

Cars
ISBN 978-1-4085-0076-7

Text by Carmel Reilly
Illustration by Luke Jurevicius
Edited by Kate McGough
Designed by Vonda Pestana
Series Design by James Lowe
Production Controller Emma Hayes
Photo Research by Corrina Tauschke
Audio recordings by Juliet Hill, Picture Start
Spoken by Matthew King and Abbe Holmes
Printed in China by 1010 Printing International Ltd

Website www.nelsonthornes.com

Acknowledgements
The author and publisher would like to acknowledge permission to reproduce material from
the following sources:
Photographs by Advertising Archive, p. 8; Age fotostock/Bartomeu Amengual, p. 10/ Grantpix, p. 13; Getty
Images/Hulton Archive/Stringer, p. 4; Istockphoto.com/Andrea Gingerich, pp. 3, 11 top; Newsphotos.com, p. 14
bottom; Newspix.com, cover, p. 1/ Mike Clarke, p. 12/ Bob Finlayson, p. 5 bottom/ Sebastian Willnow, p. 5 top;
Photolibrary.com, p. 8 top/ Voller Ernst, pp. 7, 7 bottom/ Mauritius Die Bildagentur, p. 11 bottom/ Index Stock
Imagery, p. 6/ Photolibrary.com/Science Photo library/TRL LTD, p. 14 top; Photos.com, p. 9.

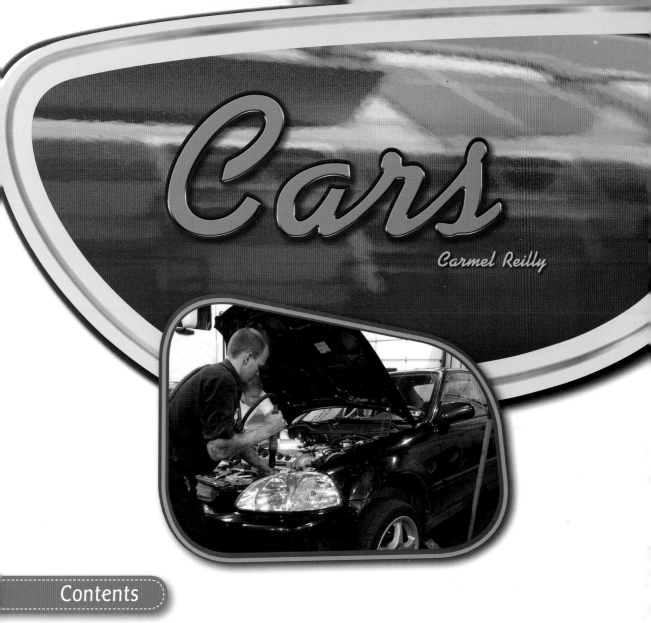

Cars

Carmel Reilly

Contents

Chapter 1   **Then and Now**   4

Chapter 2   **More Cars**   8

Chapter 3   **Good Things about Cars**   10

Chapter 4   **Bad Things about Cars**   12

Glossary and Index   16

THEN AND NOW

Cars were first made over 100 years ago.

In 1891, a car company in France
was the first company to make and sell cars.
They made five cars in their first year.

Today, car companies make
millions of cars a year.
The car industry
is one of the biggest industries
in the world.

Before there were cars,
trains were used to carry people and **goods**.
Trains could carry a lot of things,
but they had to go where there were railway lines.

People liked cars, buses and trucks
because they could go on any road any time.
A lot of the time,
people could drive themselves.

MORE CARS

Henry Ford

By the 1900s,
car companies had started up
all over the world.

In the USA, a car-maker called Henry Ford
worked out a way to make a lot of cars quickly
and sell them at low cost.

A Dashing Ford Roadster

THE words *de luxe* are a fitting description of the Ford De Luxe Roadster. In lines, colors and appointments it reflects the latest mode in a dashing sport car.

The swagger top has natural wood bows and can be raised or lowered easily and quickly. The side seat is upholstered in genuine Bedouin grain leather. The slanting windshield folds flat and is made of Triplex shatter-proof glass, as are the windshield wings. A comfortable rumble seat is provided as standard equipment. Many exposed bright metal parts are made of gleaming Rustless Steel. Fender-well is available at slight additional cost.

The Ford De Luxe Roadster is available in a variety of body colors, with an additional harmonizing color for the steel-spoke wheels. You may purchase it on economical terms through the Authorized Ford Finance Plans of the Universal Credit Company.

The New Ford Victoria

...Y FORD BODY TYPE OF DISTINCTIVE BEAUTY

...o the wide variety of Ford body types is ... Victoria. It marks a new degree of beauty

...ord Victoria are especially apparent in ...ter, lower top, the slanting windshield ...e spare wheel set at a conforming angle. ...design also in the shape and size ...imate interior arrangement.

The comfortable, deeply cushioned seats are carefully tailored and upholstered in luxurious mohair or fashionable Bedford cord, optional with the purchaser. Colors, appointments and hardware reflect the mode and manner of a custom-built car.

With all its new beauty and outstanding mechanical performance, the Ford Victoria sells at a low price. In addition, you may purchase it on convenient, economical terms through the Authorized Ford Finance Plans of the Universal Credit Company.

Because these cars did not cost much,
a lot of people could buy them.

Soon, a lot of people were driving cars.
Now, people in most countries have cars.

Chapter 3

GOOD THINGS ABOUT CARS

People saw that there were good things about cars.

People could go where they wanted very quickly.
Buses and trucks made carrying goods
and groups of people easy.

The car industry got big quickly.
A lot of people got jobs
making car parts and fixing cars.

People also got jobs making roads
for cars to drive on.
Even more people got jobs driving buses and trucks
to carry people and goods.

Chapter 4

BAD THINGS ABOUT CARS

Over time, people saw that there were also bad things about cars.

Cars take up a lot of room on the roads.
It's not always easy to find a car park.
Cars also make a lot of noise,
and they make **pollution** that can hurt people
and the **environment**.

More than anything,
millions of people around the world
have been hurt or killed in car accidents
over the years.

A lot of the bad things about cars can be worked on.

A lot of car companies are making cars that are smaller, quieter and safer.
They are also making cars that don't make as much pollution.

But one thing that will not change soon is parking. Finding a car park is never going to be easy, until car-makers make a car that can fold up.

BAY 01

Glossary

environment   the world in which we live, including the earth, sea and air

goods   things that we make, use, buy or sell

pollution   something that can harm people and the environment

Index

buses   7, 10, 11

car accidents   13

car companies   4, 5, 8

car industry   5, 11

car parks   12, 15

environment   12

Ford, Henry   8

jobs   11

pollution   12, 14

roads   7, 11, 12

trains   6

trucks   7, 10, 11